LIFESKILLS IN ACTION

MONEY SKILLS

Living on a Budget

JANE GARDNER

D0291778

LIFESKILLS IN ACTION
MONEY SKILLS

SADDLEBACK
EDUCATIONAL PUBLISHING
www.sdlback.com

All images from Dreamstime.com and Shutterstock.com

ISBN-13: 978-1-68021-000-2
ISBN-10: 1-68021-000-9
eBook: 978-1-63078-294-8

Printed in Malaysia

20 19 18 17 16   2 3 4 5 6

Money.

We all need it. We all use it.

We need money to live. To eat. To pay bills. To go places.

But how can we make sure we have enough?

Do you have a job?

The money you make is your **income**.

This is money you have coming in.

You spend money.

You buy things you want.

Pay for things you need.

These are **expenses**.

This is money that goes out.

Some spend **too much money**.

They use more money than they have.

Their expenses are more than
their income.

This is a problem. They have to ask
for help. They owe other people
money. They may have to pay back
even more money.

7

A **budget** helps.

It is a plan.

A plan to manage money in and money out.

A budget may be for a week.

Monthly Budget

1. Mortgage $1050
2. Gas $100
3. Electricity $100
4. Telephone $60
5. Internet $50
6. Food, Grocery $340
7. misc $200
   190

Or a month. Or a year.

Many people have a monthly budget.

Some budget for something they want.

A car. A trip. Jewelry.

Here is a budget.

It shows income.

It shows expenses.

It tracks money that comes in.

It tracks money that goes out.

Monthly Budget

Income

Job at Tech World	$600.00
Job at Larson's Landscapes	$240.00
Total Income	$840.00

Expenses

Fixed Expenses

Room and board	$400.00
Internet fee (my share)	$21.00
Cable TV (my share)	$15.00
Phone (my share)	$14.50

Variable Expenses

Laundry ($5/week x 4 weeks)	$20.00
Bus fare	$31.50
Clothing	$25.00
Personal care/drugstore	$15.00
Haircut	$18.00
School supplies	$20.00
Snack food ($10/week x 4 weeks)	$40.00
Entertainment ($25/week x 4 weeks)	$100.00
Total Expenses	$720.00

A budget should show **all the money** that comes in.

You may have more than one job.

You may work at a store. Mow lawns. Walk dogs.

Add up all the money you make in a month. This is your income.

Expenses...
    Rent: $700
    Cable: $125
    Cell Phone: $60
    Car payment: $250

Then add up your expenses.

Do you pay rent? Put that first.

Add in the cable bill.

Add what you pay for a cell phone.

And any other monthly bills.

These expenses are there
every month.

You can plan on them.

Some expenses **change**.

You might spend more or less on them.

Things like:

- clothes
- food
- gas
- fun

It is harder to fit these in a budget.

Do you know where your money goes?

That is the first step to making a budget.

Keep track of every dollar.

Write down everything you buy.

Use a notebook. Or an app on your phone.

Then look over the notes. See where your money went.

Income...........................$950
Expenses.......................$1,000

Look at this budget. It does not work.

There are more expenses than income.

More money is going out than coming in.

Something has to be **cut**.

A budget shows where you spend money.

Look at the expenses that change.

Find places to cut back.

Make lunch at home.

Don't drive. Walk or bike.

Find things you can
do without.

Small changes add up.

Here is an idea.

Do you like coffee?

Two cups of coffee a day cost about $10.

Most people work five days a week. Two cups of coffee each work day adds up.

That is $50 a week. Or $200 a month.

Buy only one cup each day.

You will save $100 each month!

Income $950
~~Expenses .... $1,000~~
Expenses $900

$100 in expenses cut!

Now look at this budget.

Cutting back worked.

There is money left at the end of the month.

Small changes made a **big difference**.

You don't always know when you will spend money.

Things happen. Things you don't expect.

Your car breaks down.

Your computer dies.

Your pet gets sick.

These things cost money. They affect your budget.

What can you do?

Plan for **unusual expenses**.

Be ready for surprises. How?

Set aside money. Save it.

It is not easy. But it will help.

A good budget includes **saving** some money.

The money can go in a bank.

Open a savings account.

Put some money in each month.

Watch it grow.

Saving is a good idea.

A trip with friends costs money.

So does a new car. And going to college.

These kinds of things can cost a lot.

More than you make in a month.

That is where saving comes in. It helps.

You can save up for big things.

Budgets can be hard.

Your friends are having fun.

You are watching expenses.

It can leave you feeling left out.

But keep the future in sight.

A budget will help you save.

And that helps you get things you really want.

You can save and still have fun.

Find things to do that don't cost much.

Cook dinner with friends.

Watch a movie on TV.

Swap clothes.

Go for a bike ride.

Things change.

The changes can be good.

You get a raise.

You get a new job.

You have more income.

The changes can also be bad.

You go to the dentist. Your teeth need work.

Your expenses go up.

Keep a close eye on your budget.

It can go up and down.

You may spend too much one month.

If you do, cut costs the next month.

Work toward having more income than expenses.

A budget helps you **manage money**.

There are fewer surprises.

You can make plans.

You can live your dreams.

Set a budget.

Stick to it.

You can do it!

Does budgeting pay off? That's what Curtis and his friends find out in *Road Trip*. Want to read on?

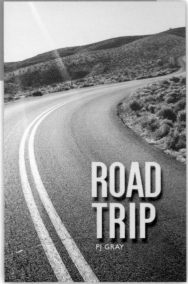

JUST *flip* THE BOOK!

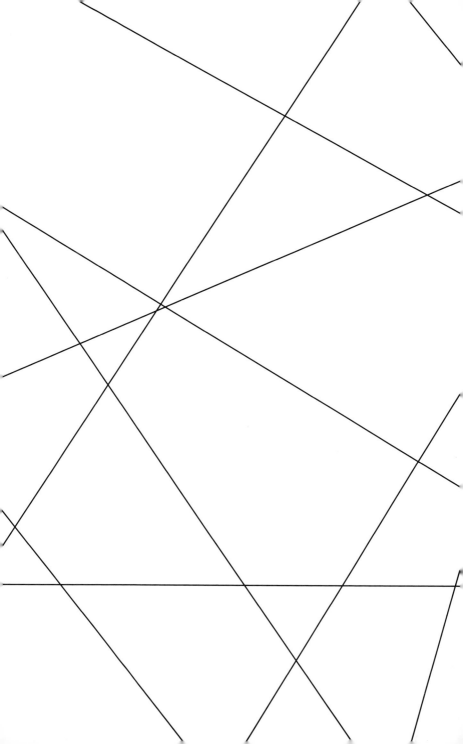

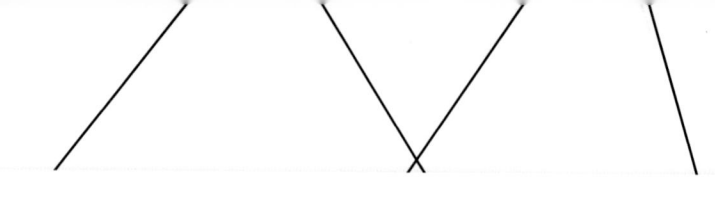

Curtis, Todd, and Ron are friends. They have been friends since first grade. They are now juniors. They go to the same high school. They also work in the same shoe store.

Curtis has a car. He saved his money to buy it. He drives Todd and Ron to school every morning. They give him gas money.

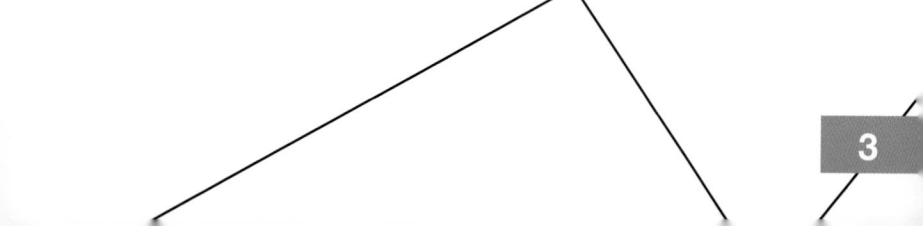

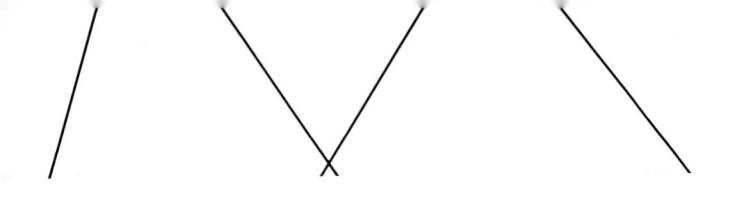

One morning, Curtis has news to share. "I want to go to Lark College," he says.

"Wow!" Todd says. "How far away is that?"

"It's about 18 hours by car," Curtis says.

"My dad lives near that school," Ron says.

"Summer is coming," Curtis says. "I want to see the college."

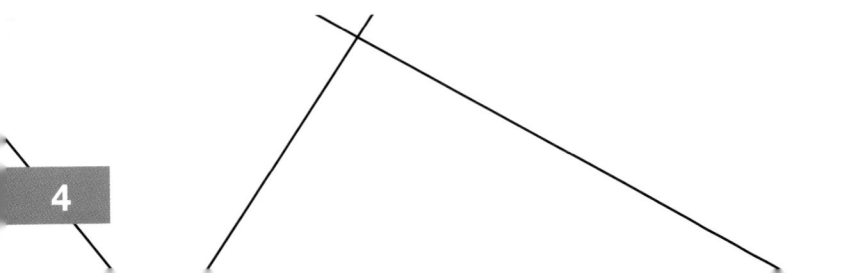

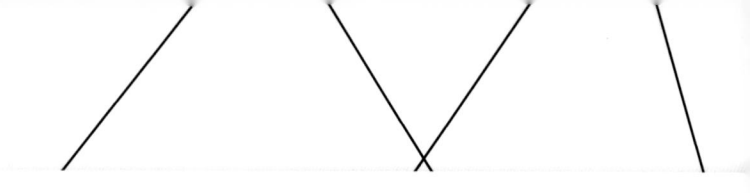

"That's a great idea," Todd says.

"How about a road trip?" Curtis asks.

"All of us?" Ron asks.

"Why not? You can see your dad. I can see the school."

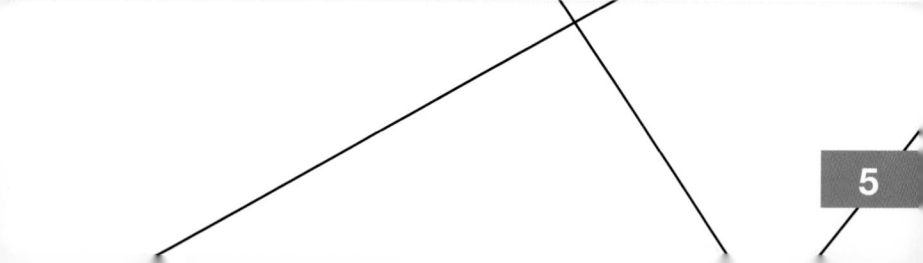

"Isn't Smith Falls near that school?" Todd asks.

"Yes," Curtis says. "It's on the way."

"We can go sky diving there," Todd says.

"What about Cleveland?" Ron asks. "Will we pass it?"

"I think so," Curtis says.

"Let's go to the Rock and Roll Hall of Fame."

"That all sounds great," Curtis says. "Let's talk about it tomorrow."

Curtis drives into the school parking lot.
He parks the car. "Let's shake on it," Curtis
says.

All three friends shake hands. "It's a deal,"
Ron says. They hear the school bell ring.

Curtis picks up Todd and Ron the next
morning. "I came up with a plan," Curtis
says. "I wrote it all down."

"Great," Todd says.

"Let's meet at lunch," Curtis says. "We can
talk about it."

Ron looks down at Todd's feet. "Todd, are those new shoes?" Ron asks.

"Yes," Todd says. "You like them?"

"Another pair of new shoes?" Curtis asks.

"Yeah. So what?" Todd asks.

"You buy a new pair every week!"

"No, I don't," Todd says. Then he smiles. "Every other week."

"Where do you get the money?" Ron asks.

"We work at the same store," Todd says. "We get a deal. Did you forget?"

"No," Ron says.

"You don't use the deal," Todd says. "You never buy shoes. You never spend money."

"So what?" Ron says. "It's good to save."

"What are you waiting for?"

Curtis looks at Todd. "Will you have the money for the trip?" he asks.

"Sure," Todd says. "No big deal."

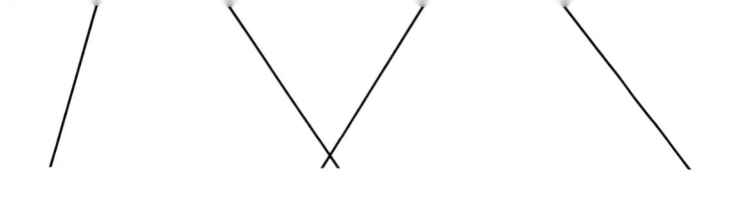

They meet in the lunchroom that day. Curtis passes papers to Todd and Ron. "I made a list of costs," he says. "Gas. Motels. Food."

Todd and Ron look at their papers.

"We can cut the costs three ways," Curtis says.

"This is more than I hoped to spend," Ron says. "Why will the trip take six days?"

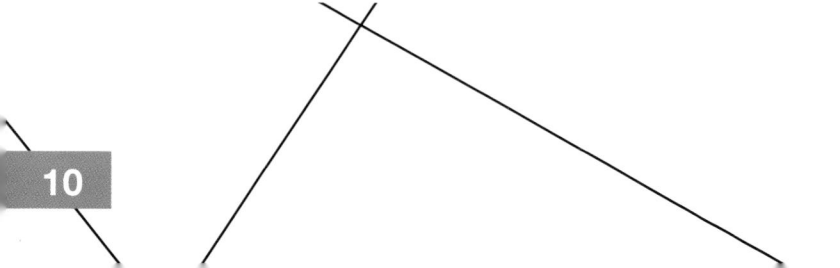

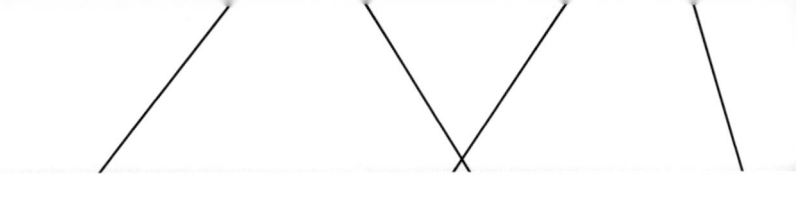

"Two days to drive there," Curtis says. "I want two days at the college. Then we have two days to drive back. That's five nights to stay in motels."

"What is your problem?" Todd asks Ron. "You have plenty of money. You never spend any of it."

"Back off, Todd," Ron says.

"Guys!" Curtis says. "Don't fight."

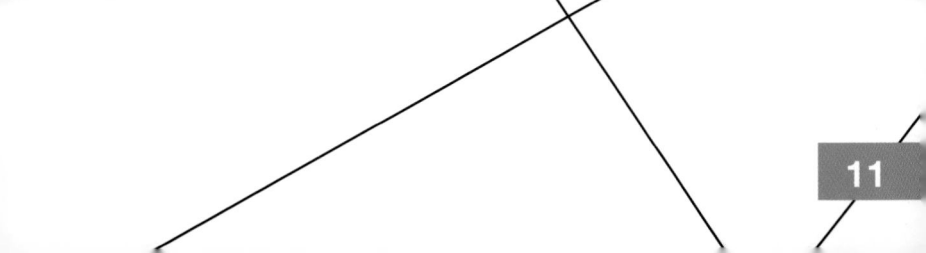

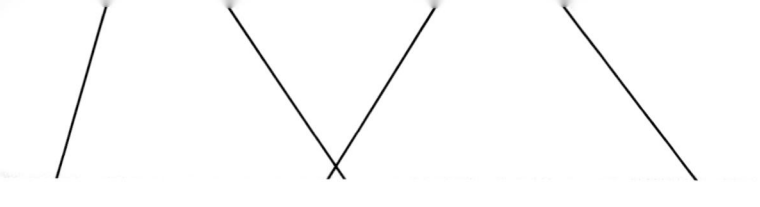

Curtis looks at Ron. "Can we stay with your dad?" Curtis asks. "That could save us money."

"No," Ron says. "He doesn't have room. He lives with his new wife and her kids. I don't like them."

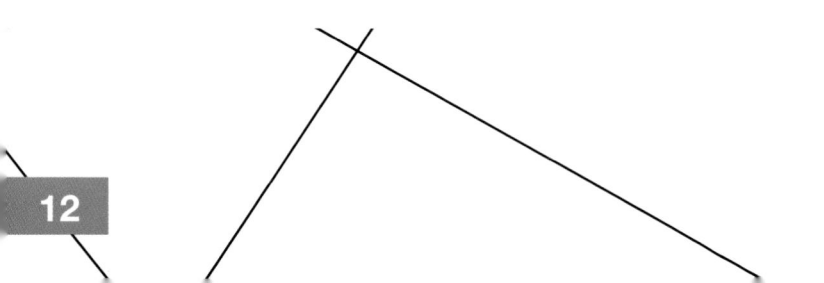

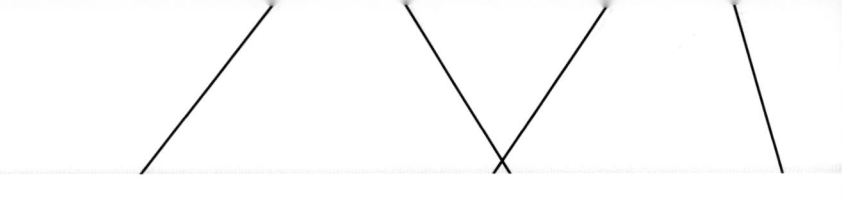

"Okay," Curtis says. "We will stick with my plan. We each have three months to save."

"Okay," Ron says.

"Cool," Todd says.

The school bell rings. Lunch is over.

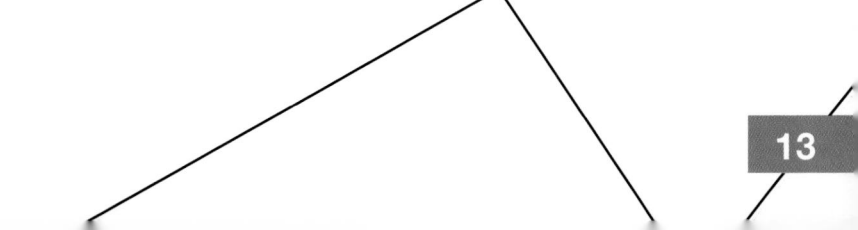

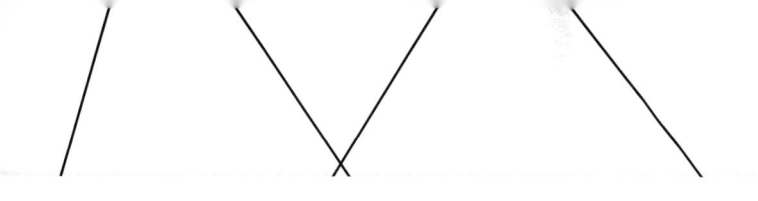

One month goes by. Curtis is trying to save money. He has a girlfriend. Her name is Jill. He meets Jill for a date.

"I want to save money for my trip," he says.

"I know," Jill says.

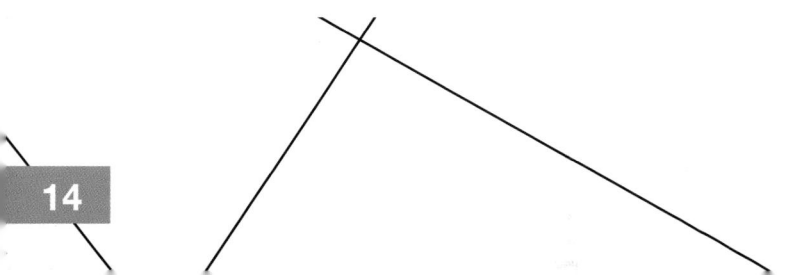

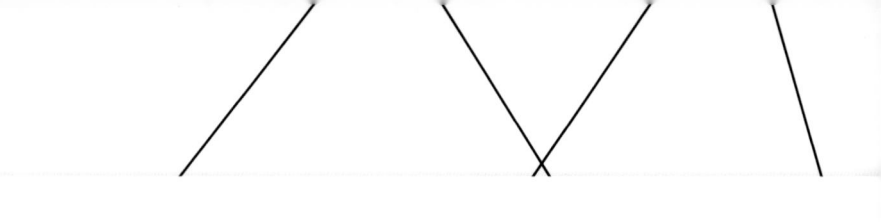

"We won't be able to eat out as much."

"Don't worry," Jill says. "We don't need to spend money to see each other."

"Thanks," Curtis says. He kisses Jill.

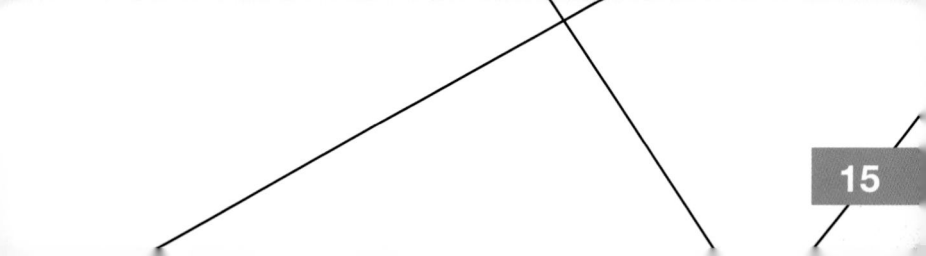

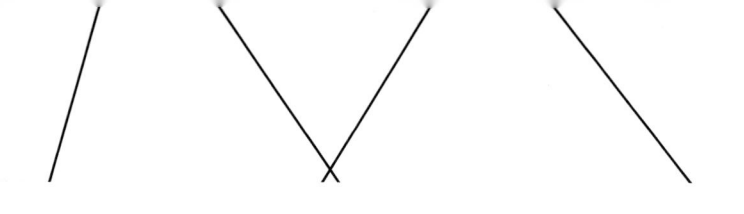

Two more weeks go by. Curtis and Ron are working at the shoe store. Ron opens boxes of new shoes.

"Those are nice," Curtis says. "I wish I could buy a pair."

"Why don't you?" Ron asks.

"I'm still saving up for the trip."

"Good for you," Ron says. "You are doing better than Todd."

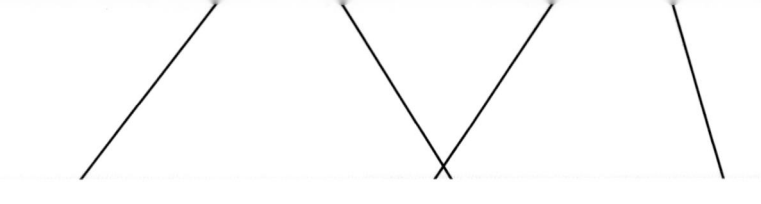

"What do you mean?" Curtis asks.

"Todd buys a new pair every week. And the boss just cut his work hours."

"I see," Curtis says.

"And he went on three dates last week," Ron says.

"What about you?" Curtis asks. "Will you have your share?"

"Don't worry about me," Ron says.

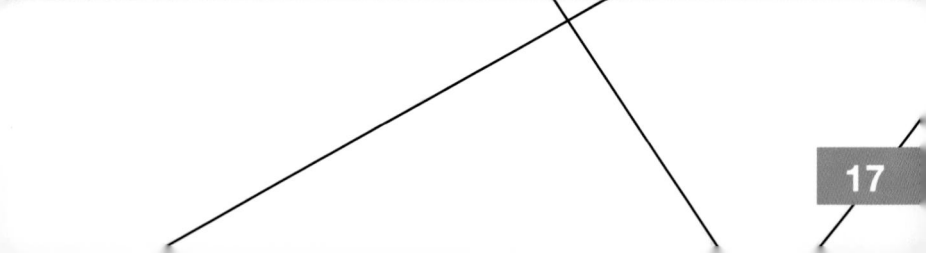

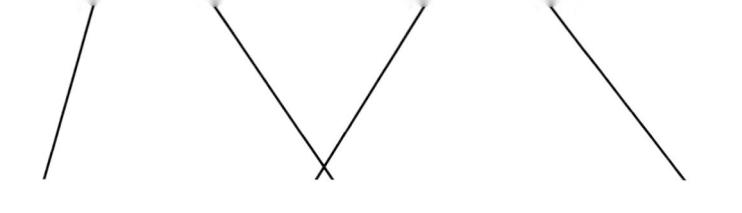

Two more weeks go by. Curtis, Ron, and Todd meet in the lunchroom. Curtis and Ron brought their lunch from home. Todd sits down with a tray.

"That is a nice shirt," Curtis says.

"You like it?" Todd asks. "I got it to match these." Todd puts his feet in the air.

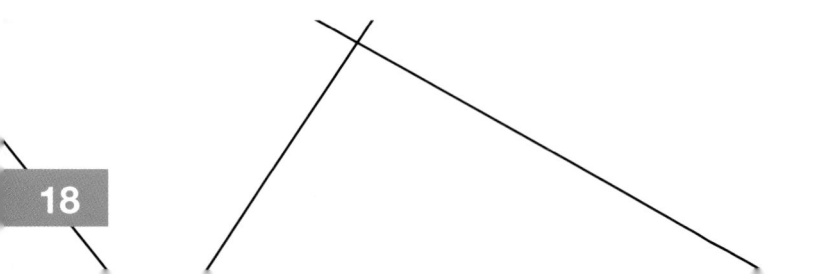

"Are those new shoes?" Ron asks.

"You like them?" Todd asks. "They glow in the dark."

"What about the trip?" Curtis asks. "Will you have the money?"

"Sure," Todd says. "Don't worry about it."

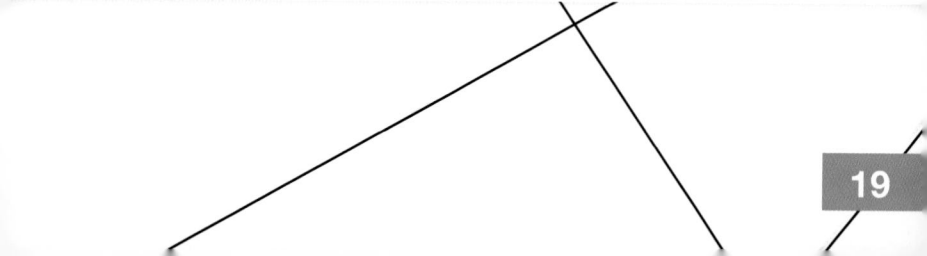

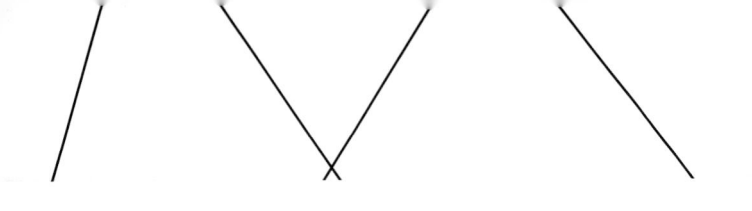

The next day Curtis is in math class. "Do any of you want a job?" Mr. Hall asks. The class is quiet. "The job pays cash," he says. "Who wants to know more?"

Curtis raises his hand.

"Okay, Curtis," Mr. Hall says. "See me after class."

Mr. Hall knows some kids. They need help with their math work. "Their parents will pay you well," Mr. Hall says. "You have to meet them after school. Three days a week until summer begins."

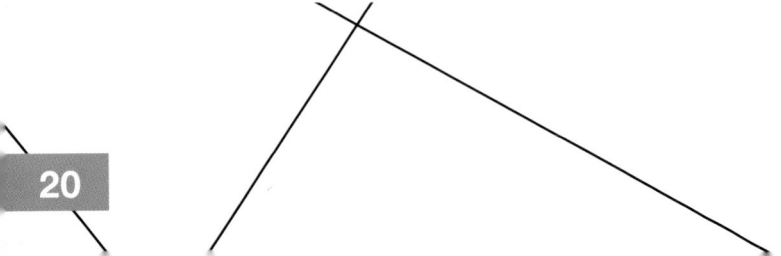

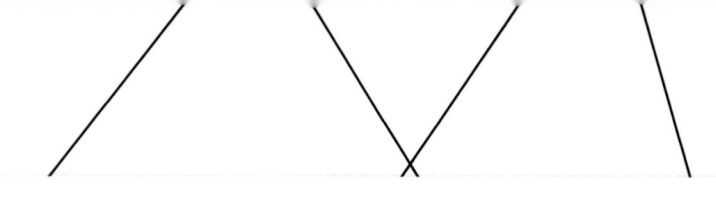

"Okay," Curtis says. He knows he can fit in the hours. He works at the shoe store two evenings a week and on weekends.

"Do we have a deal?" Mr. Hall asks.

"Deal," Curtis says. They shake hands.

Curtis is happy. Now he will have the money for the trip.

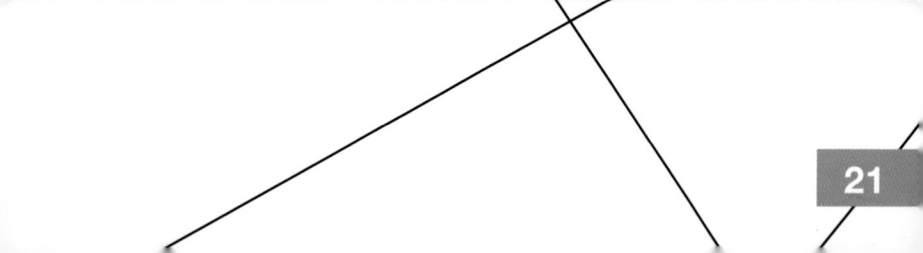

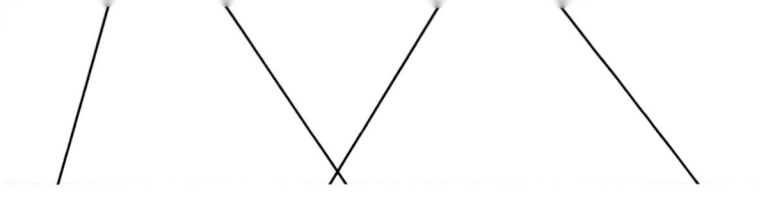

Two more weeks go by. Todd is not happy. He lost more hours from work.

Todd talks to his boss. "I need more hours. I'm going on a trip."

"You were late to work again," his boss says. "That's why I cut your hours. I should have fired you."

Todd is broke. He has no money for the trip. He does not want to tell Curtis and Ron. He goes to his dad for help.

"No!" his dad says.

"Please, Dad," Todd says. "I will pay you back."

"You still owe me money," his dad says. "I paid off your credit cards. We had to cut those cards. Did you forget?"

"No, sir."

"You will get no more money from me."

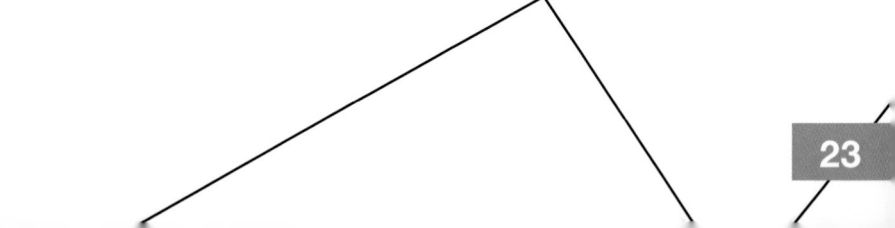

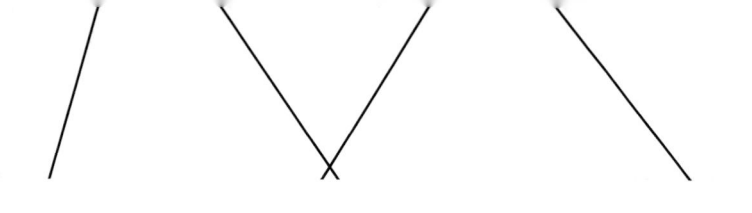

The last day of school arrives. The road trip is one week away. Curtis, Ron, and Todd meet after school.

"Are we ready for the trip?" Curtis asks.

"Yes," Ron says. "I can't wait!"

"Todd, how about you?" Curtis asks.

Todd looks down. He pushes the dirt with his new shoes.

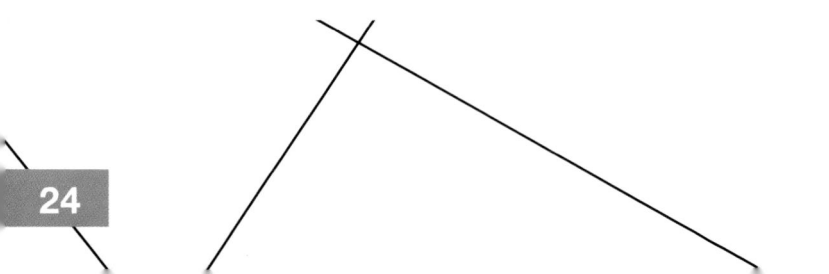

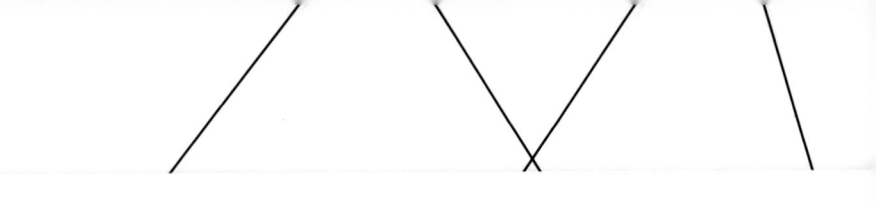

"What is it?" Ron asks Todd.

"Sorry, guys," Todd says. "I can't go. I don't have the money."

"What?" Curtis asks.

"I'm broke," Todd says.

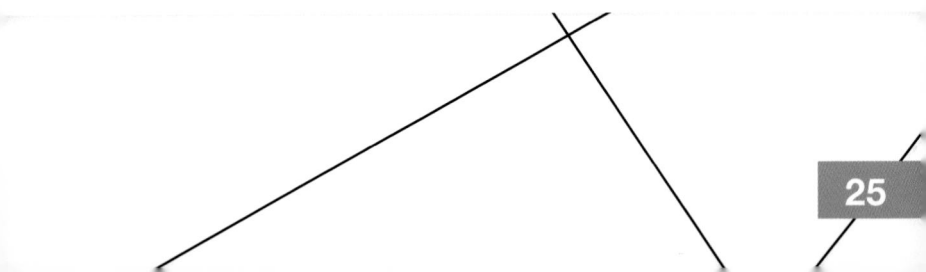

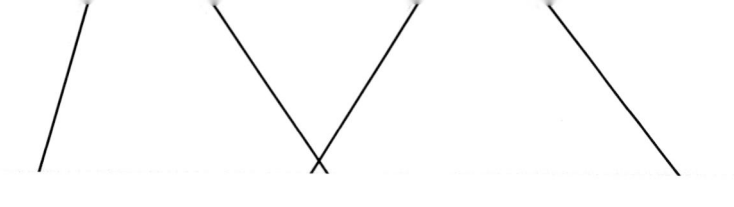

Curtis is mad. Very mad. "I knew it!" Curtis says. "We should have never asked you to go!"

"I said that I was sorry."

"Sorry?" Curtis asks.

"I know I messed up."

"We had a deal!" Curtis says. "And you broke it." Curtis turns and walks to his car.

"Curt, wait," Todd says.

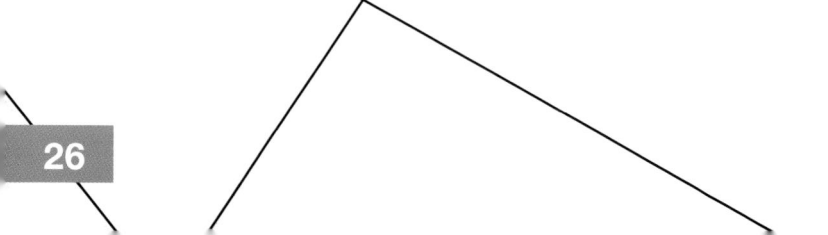

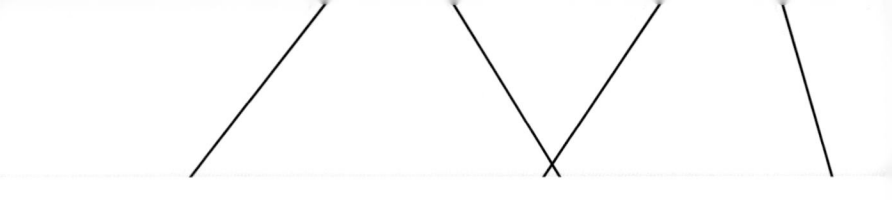

"We are done here," Curtis says. He gets into his car.

"Not cool," Ron says to Todd.

"Ron, help me out," Todd says. "I know you have the money. Cover me. I'll pay you back."

"I hope you like those shoes," Ron says. "They cost you a friend." Ron gets into the car. He and Curtis drive away.

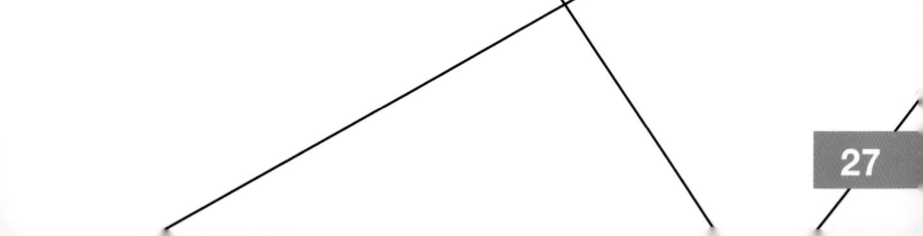

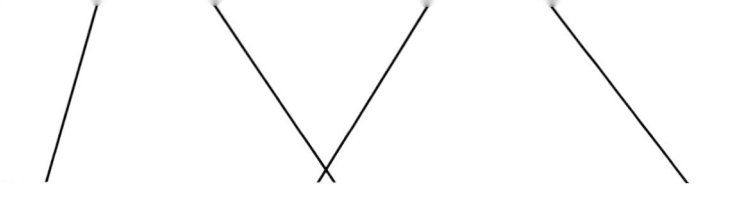

Curtis drives Ron home. They do not talk at first. Ron does not know what to say. He knows that Curtis is still mad.

Five minutes later, Curtis looks at Ron. "I guess the trip is off," he says.

"Why?" Ron asks.

"We need Todd's share of the cost."

"I have an idea," Ron says. "I will cover Todd's share."

"What?"

"This trip is a big deal to you," Ron says.
"We have to go."

"Can you afford it?" Curtis asks.

"Sure," Ron says. "Todd is right. I do like to
save money. I don't like to spend it. But I
will spend money at the right time. And I will
spend it on the right thing."

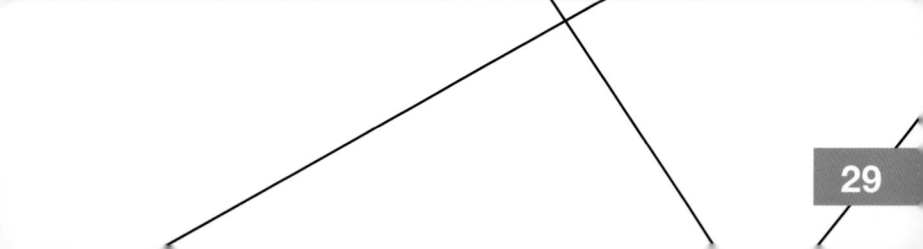

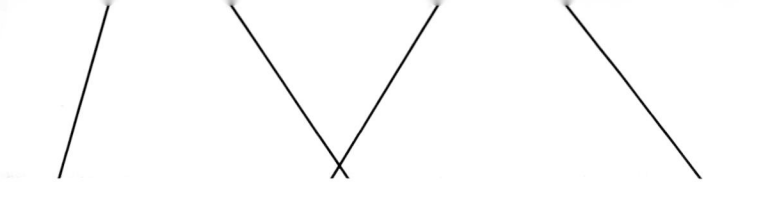

They stop at Ron's house. Ron opens the car door to get out.

"Hey," Curtis says.

Ron turns. Curtis holds out his hand.

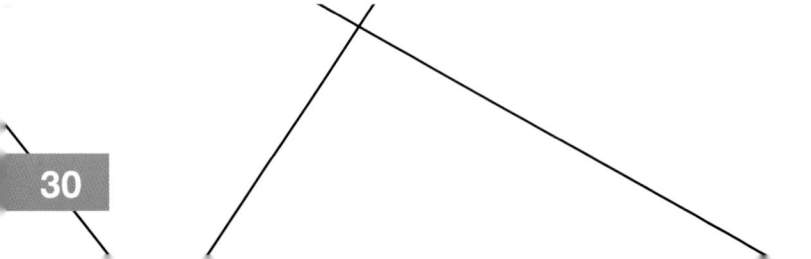

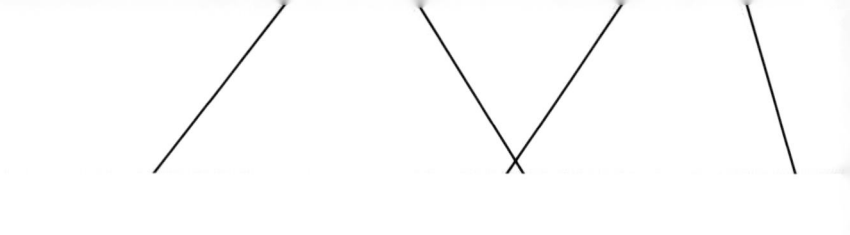

"Thanks," Curtis says with a smile.

Ron smiles back. They shake hands.

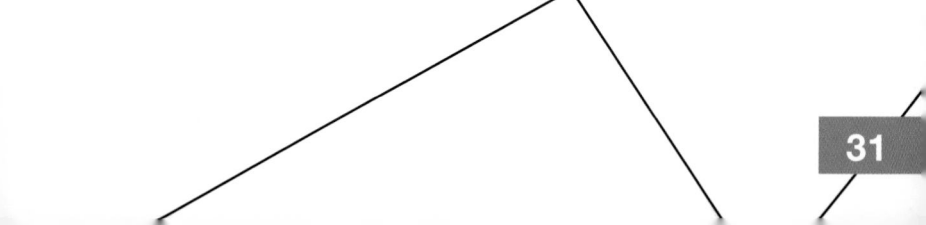

JUST *flip* THE BOOK!

JANE GARDNER

MONEY
SKILLS+
Living on
a Budget

LIFESKILLS IN ACTION

What could Todd have done to
keep his part of the deal? Find
out more about how budgeting
can help on the other side of
this book.